Being raised in a family of 10 people, eight being the total number of children, taught me to share, open my heart and sacrifice. Most importantly, it taught me to love and understand how important a brother and sister can be in my life. Through good times and bad, we became a force that could conquer anything. In my journey through life, they were always there to support me. This story brings you along, and lets you share the journey we followed. Soon, I will reach the age of 77 years young. I have experienced love, birth and laughter, sadness and death of a brother. Love for animals, nature and just slowing walking through the woods in the early morning hours, gives my day a very special meaning. Every day is a special gift. A day you can put a smile on someone's face. Life does not let you know what your journey will be. Accept each day and honor its beginning and end.

Did I become rich or poor or famous? What did I become? I became a person that no one can put a label on. I become a person that is proud of who I am. ME.

Regards: Abbey Golden,
Orillia, Ontario
Canada

This story, being true from the very beginning to the very end, is dedicated to the strength of my wonderful family. This journey travels you back in time to unveil and honor all my brothers and sisters for the courage and love that we shared. This story is a lifetime memory that will always prove to the world, that no matter what your journey will entail, your ability to resist weakness knowing courage and strength will always overcome. A loving hometown can wrap its love from strength to strength with ever increasing success to support determination and togetherness of a family. My family never gave up the fight to succeed in life. As children our favourite saying was "Stronger together we can be." "New Ways for us to smile together as one." For some, a hometown is just a place but for us children, it was part of what we were and what we have become. A caring and involved citizen in our community.

Abbey Golden

MY HOMETOWN

AUSTIN MACAULEY PUBLISHERS™

LONDON • CAMBRIDGE • NEW YORK • SHARJAH

Ordering Information
Quantity sales: Special discounts are available on quantity purchases by corporations, associations, and others. For details, contact the publisher at the address below.

Publisher's Cataloging-in-Publication data
Golden, Abbey
My Hometown

ISBN 9781685620363 (Paperback)
ISBN 9781685620370 (ePub e-book)

Library of Congress Control Number: 2022922331

www.austinmacauley.com/us

First Published 2023
Austin Macauley Publishers LLC
40 Wall Street, 33rd Floor, Suite 3302
New York, NY 10005
USA

mail-usa@austinmacauley.com
+1 (646) 5125767

Stephen Davids is a creative writing author and my writing teacher for four years. Taking his time to teach writing to many young beginner writers. His successful writing group is called "Just Write Orillia".

Also Russ Greenwood for his encouragement.

My home town was very special to me. For me, it was a memory of being born and raised in a place that will always be part of who I am and always will be with me. It is a memory that you can't buy or sell or even pretend is yours. It is like a day that you have left behind but is a day that you cherish as part of your memory. It was a different time. A hometown where the pre-planted large, overhanging trees almost overlapped the street lights. Leaving a guarded scene for modest homes with well gardened front lawns. A place people took pride in and looked after their home.

Our town at that time was a sleepy fruit-producing area with peaches, grapes, cherries, and strawberries, and many of the families lived on farms or small wartime houses. It was a working man's town. The house that you were born in, usually was the house that you would pass away in. A time when having a job and family was everything to you. If you had these two elements in your life, you could consider yourself a rich and happy man. The street I lived on contained neighbors that all knew one another; they usually knew where you worked and how often you watered your lawn. When someone was expecting a baby, they all knew and wanted to know when it would be born. It was a reason to then plan a neighborhood baby shower for the new arrival.

It was a town where you could take a deep breath of cool fresh air and hear nothing but the sound of birds and the normal sound of the early morning milkman going door to door with the help of this faithful milk wagon and horse. When I heard him coming in the morning in the wintertime, I used to run down the stairs and pull the bottles of milk into the house. I would be the first of eight children to drink the top cream off the top of the cold glass milk bottles. That was the start of a day that I hoped to be full of adventure.

I was born in the cold month of February. In the year 1945. It should have been a year of celebration, to a point it was. A year the war was finally over. But a year when many lives were lost. A time to reflect on how the world had suffered and had been thrown into turmoil. Food was scarce. Butter and sugar, non-existent. A time when seeing the delivery of a letter to your home by a delivery boy could be a disastrous news of a soldier's death.

When you heard a knock on your back door, you knew it was a roaming father asking for a food handout. These were caring, hard-working men without a job, usually traveling by train. They usually had a home somewhere but were out of work. They traveled to find a job so they could support their family and themselves. They were not hobos; they cared enough for their families at home to endure this hard, desperate existence. My mother was extra kind to these gentlemen, giving them any extra sugar and supplies for them to take home.

To this day, I remember my mother giving me a plastic bag of white margarine with a large, red fluid spot in the middle of the bag. She would say squeeze and get the bag to look like yellow. Beat that margarine bag up to look like butter.

It was not often that us kids would be told to actually do something that was totally fun for us.

I was now the third born in our family; Carl was born first, then Betty came along. My name is Abbey. Now I have an older brother and sister to teach me the good and bad things I should be learning, but hopefully, they will just teach me the good things. My older brother would set the tone for being a helper in the neighborhood. When walking, neighbors would walk by our house with an armful of groceries, almost too much for them to carry. My brother would step in and spring into action. Taking some of those bags out of the arms of an overly heavy burdened housewife could lend him a nice nickel or a few pennies quite often it did.

In the wintertime, we would grab our snow shovels and make sure we knew where the oldest people in the neighborhood lived. Any extra spending money quickly turned into a quick trip to the nearest candy store, where most of it was spent. When, on occasion, if both parents would be absent for some emergency reason, the neighbors would take turns watching over us and feeding us until the grandparents showed up to babysit. For me, that is what a real family would do. It always gave us kids asense of security at all times.

Xmas time in our home town was simple, warm, and friendly. It brought the country into our small town in an exciting and anticipating way. Especially for small children, school Xmas programs and church programs were well attended. Of course, it was a busy time for all. Sons and daughters making their way home to embrace family and friends. Real Xmas trees were the only ones that you could bring home to decorate. Presents were bought from your neighborhood stores. Large shopping malls and shopping online did not exist.

Our Xmas was just what our parents could manage to provide. For our family it meant, we could pick any stocking we wanted to hang. Of course, we picked a large, stretchy Hockey stocking; each child received one present each. You wouldn't think of traveling to a large city to shop. Some of our neighbors had cars then. But a lot of our neighbors didn't. They would walk to their place of employment and walk to the nearest grocery store. They were more than happy to spend their Xmas money in the small town where they lived.

The time came that Xmas was fast approaching, preparing for Xmas dinner was always a very important part of our Xmas celebration. The turkey usually took the most time to prepare and was the most important part of our Xmas dinner. My mother always told me this story that I often tell my grandchildren today. It was an unusually quiet day at our home; I was home with only Abbey. I was busy in the kitchen starting the preparations. My daughter Abbey was in the living room, playing with her favorite toys. Wandering into the kitchen, she was watching me thoroughly wash the large turkey in the kitchen sink. Of course, it was a raw, skin-covered bird with its two legs splashing in the rinse water. My daughter suddenly screamed with fright, running straight into her bedroom. I was stunned at her behavior; I left the sink and ran after her. She was frightened, with tears running down her chubby cheeks. I said, "What is the matter?"

She said, "Mommy, did that animal try to hurt you?"

Once I realized what she had observed, I could now understand why she interpreted, as a young child, what she did. Thinking the turkey was an animal that she had never seen before in the kitchen sink could hurt her mommy. I had to try and piece her half crying childlike recall together. My daughter was afraid I was being attacked by the turkey that I was rinsing in the kitchen sink.

I said, "Abbey, that animal is our special meat for our Xmas dinner. Mommy was just washing him; he wanted us to eat him on Xmas day. He told me his name is 'Charlie.' 'Charlie' wanted to share himself with us. He was a friendly animal and would never hurt anyone. Come with Mommy and see and help me stuff 'Charlie' and then we will put him in the oven to cook."

So me and my daughter Abbey did just that. My daughter was so excited now that she had helped Mommy prepare 'Charlie' for his trip to the oven to cook. She returned to the living room where she answered the phone, which I didn't hear ringing. It was my mother. I guess my mother asked for me, but Abbey loved to talk on the phone. She told my mother that Mommy was busy cooking 'Charlie' in the oven and hung up. About half an hour later, my mother called back, I answered. My mother said, "What's this about you putting some man in the oven, called 'Charlie'?" Of course, I laughed and laughed and explained.

Now my three-year-old is a 44-year-old mother herself, and she tells that same story to her daughter, and it continues even when I still prepare Xmas Dinner today. I always mention, "Come and see how Charlie looks, cooked in my roasting pan."

After our Xmas dinner, we would grab our toboggans and ice skates, run out the door, and be gone most of the day. When I think back, those were some of the best Xmases that I ever had. The greatest gift for us was family and being part of it. I was now the third born in our family. I now had an older brother Carl and an older sister, Betty. My mother and father would say, now you have someone to teach you the good and bad things in life.

I'm not saying that our home town neighborhood was a perfect, caring, kind haven. Far from it. For some of our neighbors, it took a lesson or two to tame them down. When it comes to hot tempers and for them to get their own way. Of course, there would be small disputes. I remember our neighbor said he saw his new neighbor chasing another man with a hose and watering him down.

My oldest brother Carl would find himself in trouble. He only thought he was doing a good deed. He had overheard the neighbor talking to another man, saying he wished he had time to repaint his garage door. Well, some small kids have big ears. Thinking he would get extra money. My brother one day walked into an open garage, grabbed the best color of purple paint he had ever seen. He would have the time to repaint the neighbors' garage door and probably would get some extra money for doing it. Well, my eight-year-old brother, Carl, ended up painting three-quarters of the garage door without anyone noticing. The men in the neighborhood were all at work. The wives were all inside their homes.

My brother did earn some money for repainting the garage, but this time he and the owner worked together to repaint it. Back in those days, that would be something the owner and the neighborhood could laugh about. Using common sense and understanding why it happened, they were able to come to a good and laughable agreement. But that was a good thing my brother had attempted to do; he also had his mischievous side to him.

My open-minded, unpredictable brother often finds himself in a situation that seems normal in every way to him. But it usually gets him in trouble with our family and others.

One day our three- and four-year-olds had been separated from the crowd of mothers and put in the back room with toys for them all to play with. It was a large baby shower, and it lasted about two hours. Time for everyone to leave. They opened the door to the babysitting room to find that my brother had climbed up to the bathroom cabinet, took his dad's razor, and shaved off at least one eyebrow each of the children he was babysitting. There sat two three-year-olds with only one eyebrow. The third child, a four-year-old girl, sat there happy, holding some of the hair in her hands that my brother had cut from her head.

Yes, there were screams, but there was also laughter. Knowing the eyebrows would grow back. The haircut was a very upsetting problem. The three children were all checked over to see what else he had attempted. The hair would grow back. All three mothers said, "It's our fault. They were just too quiet in there. We all should have checked on them." One half of the four-year-old's hair was cut short; he didn't have time to start on the other half of her hair on her head. My brother thought he had done a great job, couldn't understand why everyone was upset.

Well, from then on, that story circulated throughout the whole neighborhood for months. My brother, age seven at that time, was kept busy raking leaves and doing small jobs for the mothers of the three children. This was the brother that was always curious and not afraid of doing what he thought was right. I guess he had watched his dad shave with the razor and the only hair he could see on their faces were the eyebrows. As far as him giving the four-year-old girl a haircut, he just wanted to see how it would look.

As children, our day was not complete until we could gather as a neighborhood group and talk over our day with each other. We would exchange our adventures with each other, sometimes good, other times not so good. Any new changes or additions to our neighborhood we all had to know about. Until the streets lights went on was the only sign that we as children should head for home. That is usually when you could see the parents yelling out their doors for us to come home. Snowball throwing, tree climbing, riding our bike, building your exclusive kids hid out, baseball games, soccer, skipping rope, and running games, only played a small portion how we spent our adventures days.

I remember me, my brother and my sister stayed out after the street lights went on. But this day, we had permission. The five men that played instruments from the Salvation Army had gathered around the bottom of the street light pole. That was exciting; we just had to be part of it. We loved the music, their uniforms. We danced to their music, clapped our hands. I'm sure they were happy that we gave them attention and appreciated them. Boy, it sure was fun to be a kid back in those days.

Our elderly neighbor across the street had two big matching pear trees on her front lawn, which all of us and the neighbor kids were eying until those pears got ripe. Well, that time had come, and we were all ready to climb one of those pear trees and start picking. We knew the lady that lived there was old and fragile. If we got caught halfway up that tree, we had heard and seen how she waved a cane at the kids before. Were we willing to get hit just to taste those mouthwatering pears? Well, we sat there and pondered our fate.

So we looked for the longest broom handle that we could find and would swing and hit the branches until the pears dropped. Well, that old lady must have been watching through her living room window. I guess she thought that someone could get hurt trying to get those pears, and she was not in a position to climb those trees herself. She was smart; she must have called her sons to come with ladders and baskets and climb up those two trees and pick those pears. All of us kids sat there and watched and said to ourselves, there go all those mouthwatering pears, but no! That sweet, old lady took one basket for herself and had those two men give us, the bunch of kids watching, a whole basket for us and our families. She was smart and nice.

Now, as a family of five, we as children realized that we were not rich by any means. Compared to other families, we realized we were struggling at times. My father did have a job, but not always. He was a layout technician and sometimes had to travel to get a job. He and my mother had times when they were not happy. Another sister was now added to our family, just two years after I was born. Her name is Cheryl. Her birthday would also be in February. July must have been a boom month for conception. We were now a family of six. Our neighbors, of course, had another reason to have another baby shower. Back in those days, it was normal to have a large family. Sunday afternoon, when everyone normally rests, seemed to be a normal time for conception to take place. Don't forget there wasn't TV. Back in those days, in fact, we didn't even have a dial phone.

We did have an old wooden stand-alone radio that we would all sit around and listen to *Mr. and Mrs. North* or a cowboy story. Have times changed! I sometimes think back to those days, that technology and pushing for a more advanced future has taken away our simple one-on-one communication skills to a new low. Society now realizes that cell phones, computers, and other new technologies have taken away our need to communicate on a one-to-one basis. Our ability to use problem-solving techniques has no need in this world. Technology will do it for us. Why learn to talk to a person on a one-to-one basis; I can use my cell phone to talk to someone. Well, enough on the changes that you and I can now see and use to be part of this new world.

Exercise back then: you did your own exercise, just by working each day, in the garden or a factory, or on a farm. We handled it in our own way. Many areas of the town back then contained small, city-owned parks that contained baseball diamonds. It was a treat to find a baseball game in session; you could sit in the bleachers and see a real game in person, it wouldn't cost you a penny. Most of these games were played in the summer, after supper. The bleachers were usually full of interested, enthusiastic people cheering and yelling that you could hear halfway down the block.

We had a neighbor that I think, every time he had a fight with his wife, he would grab baseball bats and balls, and he would head to the playground area of the Catholic School, which had a baseball diamond. Calling all the neighborhood kids, we all would follow him to the Catholic School. We would happily play baseball, young and old; sometimes, other adults would join in. This would last about one hour or maybe two. It all depended on how exciting the game would get. And, of course, how long he was away from the house. How long it would take his wife to calm down. But us kids always loved to join in. For us, it was another exciting adventure.

In a small town back then, you will always find baseball neighborhood diamonds with bleachers that always seem full in the heat of the summer. The love of baseball is and always will be a game that draws children and adults into a healthy way of staying fit. There is always the smell of hot dogs cooking and freshly popped popcorn in the air. It offers parents a chance to work together as a team is very important in any work environment. A story that my brother, Carl, lived through we often tell to young children starting out, not knowing too much about baseball.

This is Carl's story: I was on a softball team, and I was not happy because I never could hit the baseball when I was at-bat. I was always ready to make myself set to hit that ball, but I always missed it. I'm always striking out. I run the fastest, I catch the ball all the time, but I'm afraid they now call me Carl, the strike-out kid. I try so hard; I practice, watch what the other kids do, I dream it. But I never seem to connect with the ball that is pitched to me. I shiver when it's my turn to go to bat.

My two friends play baseball on different teams, and they are good batters; they have worked with me to help me and give me good advice. But I still wait too long to hit that ball. Why I wait too long, I don't know. I want to be the best player on my baseball team. But I strike out every time I'm up to bat. I know at that time, I have let my other players down. When I know my mom and dad are sitting in the bleachers, I even try harder. It was the last baseball game of the season. My team has one player on the third base, one player on the second base; we just need two more points to win. The thing I dreaded the most was happening; it was my turn up to bat. I was sweating and lowering my head; I would understand if the coach changed the lineup. He called me over to talk, "Carl," he said, "I was going to have Devon take your place at bat, but I have faith in you; I want you TO GET MAD! Swing that bat as hard as you can, picture it, Carl, a home run so far that the fielders will have to run a while to get it."

Shivers went up and down my back; *I have to hit it this time, for sure.* Now I'm REAL MAD! The pitch came, I NEVER TOOK MY EYE OFF THAT BASEBALL! I'M MAD! I swung that bat, the hardest I have ever done. I heard a loud CRACK! The crowd cheered, *Did I hit it?* The crowd was yelling, HOME RUN! I started to run for first; *Did I really hit the ball?* The third. The base runner ran home. The second base runner made home. I was passing third base; *Could I really do it?* I am the fastest runner on our team. I could see home base. I was still in a haze when I finally realized what I had done. The people in the bleachers were on their feet clapping. *I did it!* My team and my parents lifted me on their shoulders. I had overcome my fear; I hit a fabulous home run and won the game. My sister loved the story I told her. She said to me, "It only takes one person to believe in you. But you have to also believe in yourself." Abbey, my sister, said, "I love you, Carl; you are my baseball hero."

In April and May, our home town area would have quite a bit of rain, sometimes thunder and lightning. The rain never bothered us kids; we would run and put our bathing suits on and run out into the rain—the heaviest, the better. But we were not allowed to go out when it was thundering. On those real warm, sticky days, we would head to the only swimming pool that the city owned three to five blocks away. There were no individual privately owned pools back then. During the whole summer, we as brothers and sisters often made that trip. Sometimes together, sometimes by ourselves. We had no fear of abduction back then, it was a different time. The pool offered individual swimming Lessons for free. Anything free, us kids would consider taking. What we didn't know was these individual swimming lessons had to take place early in the morning, before the pool opened, and before the pool was heated. Wow, that water was cold!

Even in the summer, wearing our bathing suits and having to climb into a swimming pool, where the water hasn't been heated. Wow! That was a challenge. But as a brother and two sisters, we were determined to conquer and finish the course because it was free, and it was another adventure we had acknowledged.

As children, we were always looking for new adventures. Playing at our school on a Saturday, we noticed a man and two boys playing yo-yos. This was something new and exciting; we had never seen yo-yos before. They were throwing them up in the air and swinging them around. Back and forward. They were leaving the hand and flying up in the sky and then returning to the start. How amazing was that! We just had to investigate. They had so many different plays that they showed us. One of these boys was from the 'Boys and Girls Club.' A new club that we, as kids, just didn't know about. They were not in our neighborhood. But not that far away from our neighborhood. We watched with wild interest. The man asked us if we would be interested in joining the boys and girls club. We inched closer to where the crowd of kids had now gathered. We said, "What do you do to join? What do you do there?"

He said, "All you have to do is get permission from your parents. We have lots of fun, not like school. We play games, we decorate, help the community. You can come after school and join us."

We asked how much money does it cost?

He said no money, but we might need you to peel potatoes for our cooking class.

We asked if we had to learn to play yo-yos, like the boy that we were watching. He said, "No, come as you are, and we will make sure that we take care of you. We will join you in with other kids to have fun, fun, and more fun."

He had permission slips with him, and I took three. The boy that was a real good yo-yo player, the other boy, and him were there to recoup children for this new boys and girls club to get started and established. What an unexpected adventure for us kids, my brothers and sisters, we were always looking to have more fun. This was happening right in front of us. Racing home, we had a grand story to tell. After listening to our story, our parents checked around the neighborhood to find out this new club was opening. Our parents signed the permission slip, but my mother would attend with us on our first time attending this club.

So after school, you could always find us at the boys and girls club. I guess the community was finding it needed a safe place for children to play. Couples were having large families with lots of kids. So their club filled up in no time. So kids from all surrounding areas found it a wonderful place to gather. We learned to share, care for, and work together as a community group of children to better our community in many ways.

We attended the Protestant School, grades kindergarten to grade six. Our school contained a large, grassed playground, one side for the girls, one side for the boys, our playground was so big, it also contained a baseball diamond, we played hopscotch, skipping, the daring marble games and any other games we could think of. Those were the times I cherished the most—such a happy break from school work. Before and after school, we would be allowed to cross the street to the candy lady, a lady that sold penny candy for a living; if we had pennies, that's where they ended up.

Our other highlight was field day, a day that if you were rich or poor, you had to participate, but I welcomed and looked forward to this event because being poor didn't matter in this event—it would only judge our ability, and I wanted to win as many red ribbons as I could.

I was always at my best on that day, and I sure did win many red (first place) ribbons. I distinctly remember in my grade four class school picture that was always taken as a class picture, all of us standing side by side together. I had refused to take off all my field day, winning red ribbons, I had pinned to my blouse for the class picture, and my teacher finally let me keep them on. Only a few memories such as this really remain with me to this very day.

There were other exciting events that us kids can remember, every September our town would have a parade, it was called 'The Grape and Wine Festival Parade.' This parade would be honoring all the crops of grapes and peaches picked in our area. All of our family used to line up and get a good seat. We would never miss seeing that parade.

In the fall, one of our most looked forward to events was 'The Fall Fair.' This was where the city and country met. A fair that everybody looked forward to every year. Driving down the country road leads us to a wonderful, busy parking area, where a welcoming clown directs us to a spot to park our car. You hear and feel the excitement of the fall fair and watch the Ferris wheel circulating in the nippy, fall air as then the sunshine suddenly peeks through.

From our parking area, the music and the smell of cotton candy, popcorn, and hot dogs already fill your senses. The sight of the sky-high Ferris wheel makes your head tilt back, and watch its circular, colorful rotation; it is a familiar sight. We gathered our thin fall jackets and sweaters because we intended to spend the whole day at the fall fair, which you looked forward to attending all summer. Some of our family made an earlier trip here to bring our prize vegetables, fruit, and homemade pies to display and try and win a prize for their product. The sunshine we all hoped for surrounded us, but the air was still fresh, chilly, and fall-like.

We approached the ticket booth that had a lineup of excited people to pay for their entry. The music, the sound of midway rides, and the usual sound of the game owners yelling their appeals to come and play their games filled the crowded area. The backdrop of the games was hung and tacked up with every colorful kind of stuffed animal that you could imagine.

All the games were side by side, with each appeal to play, could be heard a fair distance away. Of course, we played a few; that is what you do when you're at a Community Fair. We thought we could all win, but only one of us succeeded in winning a stuffed animal. But we all had fun and joked with the owner. The smell of all the carnival food filled the air. You could not turn down some of those delicious treats even though you had already eaten before we left the house. So we decided to indulge, but all of us had to participate, and we dug into the hot corn dogs, extra thick pizza, gravy, and French fries, and fresh caramel apples, with apple cider and lemonade to wash it down. Because we all joined in that meant, we only had ourselves and our temptation to blame. Everyone there was in a playful and happy mood—the fresh air was so good to breathe in.

We suddenly heard a big, loud bang, above all the other normal noise at the fairgrounds. It was the Demolition Derby just practicing. We decided to all meet at that start time. That would be a little later in the day. We still had so many things to partake in and enjoy and look at.

Every area that we entered concentrated on involving children to blow bubbles with clowns, hula hoop with them, and cowboy roping fun with them. This made every area of the fall fair keep people in a fun and happy mood.

We reached the inside area that displayed prize-winning flowers, fruit and vegetable growers, and pastries. The next building housed and displayed small animal contests, involving rabbits, guinea pigs, mice, and exotic birds. There was just so much to see and do. We also took a quick bench break; at least the adults did; the teenagers ran off somewhere to meet up at an agreed time and place.

They had pony rides just outside the second building to keep the young children occupied. Besides that, they had the cattle and goat competition. Each entrant was so proud of each animal they had raised from birth. Suddenly, there was a breakaway; a goat had pulled a lady's bright, red scarf off her neck and ran away with it. Someone should catch him if they can. We all stood there in amazement, this goat became the center of attention, and none of us could catch him. He was just too fast for everyone.

Everyone was trying to catch him, running with that lady's red scarf in his mouth, not a care in the world. For the goat, it was pure Fall Fair fun. The goat had gathered such a crowd—the crowd was hoping he would never get caught. He had everybody laughing.

We couldn't miss the old equipment pull and Demolition Derby. We were always looking forward to that interesting display. So we had just finished watching it and took a look at our watch. Suddenly our teenagers showed up. They had backtracked and bought cotton candy to munch on. I find it hard to believe their stomach had room for it. It was time for the Demolition Derby. Our teenagers would never miss that.

This was our last event, and the day had been a long, enjoyable, fun day. Everyone loves to watch this event.

The bleachers were jam-packed full. The people were standing in front of the three-story wire backstop, in front of the lower bleacher seats.

They were playing happy, action-packed music because they still needed time to line up the cars. Now they were announcing and showing each car, one by one. The first car was called DERBY DAISY; the driver wore a long blond wig. The crowd clapped and waved back; he quickly made a fast figure eight with a cloud of dust filling the air.

Then came STEP ASIDE CLYDE, a black car with about half of it missing. I didn't think that one would ever win, there was so much of it gone. Well, you never know. It all depended on what was under the hood. Then came a real junker. It was a car made with a whole bunch of different parts. They were calling him the CRUSHER. The CRUSHER made a quick turn with smoke coming from its engine and a cloud of dust for the audience to breathe in. Wow, what a dusty area for these cars to crash and bang in. Talk about noise; the cars attacked each other with a desire to win that trophy. Each car backed up and crashed together with a real vengeance, some cars I could not believe that they were still drivable; they crashed until the last surviving car, what was left of it, circled the winning spin ride, holding the black checkered flag, with a smile and a dust-covered face. It was the CRUSHER that won the prize and trophy.

Even though we had the odd outing that our family never missed, like the fall air, we were still struggling financially. Our family adding more children seemed to not only make us more of a larger unit to keep together, but we also found it just the opposite; it seemed to require more of a struggle to maintain. It took extra care and work to keep us happy and comfortable as a family. Problems were increasing, and arguments began to tear my parents apart.

My father had to go to the United States to get work. He only came home on the weekends, leaving my mother carrying the whole load of worry and work. Mothers didn't work an outside job back in those days. So it was only one salary that carried my family financially. One day it certainly played a major part in my mother leaving us alone and going to live with her mother temporarily. Mine and my brothers' and sisters' worlds fell apart. My older brother and sister tried to keep things together, but they could only do so much. My father came home and found her gone. I'll never forget the day he had my brothers and sisters in the car; I hid under the bed. I could hear him calling my name. I didn't answer.

After my father called my name four or five times, I realized I could not survive alone; I ran to the car. My father had to return to work in the States; he had no choice but to drive us to the Children's Aid Society, where he explained the situation. We were separated as brothers and sisters. Torn apart, not knowing how we depended on each other for strength and closeness. I stood in a room by myself with tears coming down my face. In the same room, there was a group of ladies sitting at typewriters doing office work. One of those ladies called me over to her. She asked my name. She let me type it on her typewriter. I'm sure she realized how traumatized I was at that time.

My innermost feelings were the loss of the comfort that my brothers and sisters always instilled in me. Now it was me alone to face what I didn't know was ahead of me. Not only had I lost my brothers and sisters to comfort me, but now my mother and father had also been taken from me. My head bowed in shame, and tears rolled down my face. Those next days and nights, I don't remember too much. I guess I blocked most of this nightmare from my memory. If it would have been happy memories, I'm sure I would have remembered them.

I think we were in the care of the Children's Aid Society for six weeks. My memory of being separated from my brothers and sisters must have been blocked out. The only thing I can remember is being brought home in a car and united with my mother. My mother ran to the car with open arms; it took a while to mend the tear in my heart, being taken away from my home and my brothers and sisters. Our family situation, for now, was calm and happy. But new changes were being implemented into and around our home.

With four girls in our family, it took a lot of time to do our hair in the morning. Especially the girls that went to school each day.

Back in those days, long hair was the style, and for young girls, braids were a must. One on one side of the head, the other braid on the other side of the head with bangs running across the forehead. And bangs, it seemed always needed to be cut. Well, I guess my mother and father were trying in their own way to make it easier for my mother to speed up and lessen the time it took to get us girls ready for school in the morning. So their solution was for my father to march us all up to the end of the street, where John the barber had cut hair year after year, for the past ten to twenty years. Nothing was told to us girls; we thought we were taking a trip to say Hi to the barber and watch my father get his hair cut.

That was what we as girls thought. Well, that was a thought that was the farthest from the truth I have ever thought. We entered the barbershop to be greeted by John, the barber. He instructed my dad to put me in the barber chair. I said, "What are you up to?"

My dad said, "All four of you need your hair cut."

I said, "Mom usually cuts our hair." The long hair past our shoulders was now cut very short, one inch above our ears. We left that barbershop, looking like two Dutch girls. We looked like that girl on the front of the Dutch cleaner. Our hair being very thick, stood out about two inches from the side of our head. So this was the time-saving theme that my parents had thought up.

Our family being five people now, meal time also took quite a bit of time. We often ate a lot of starchy food. My mother could put together a meal from almost anything. Macaroni and spaghetti, filling food. If we were hungry and told her, she would peel a raw potato or carrot and tell us to munch on it. I have to give my mother a lot of credit. She had the strength and determination to try to continue to raise her children and still be positive in her outlook. Eating a lot of potatoes meant it always took a lot of time to prepare.

I remember our dad coming home from the United States; he presented a gift to my mother. Back in those days, I don't know where he got it. But he presented my mother with a pressure cooker. He knew a lot of people that worked in the restaurant business. This pressure cooker was the oddest-looking large pot that we had ever seen, with a large dial pressure valve attached to its lid. Steam would escape the lid and the pot made funny, hissing sounds. We, as kids, always stood clear of that funny-looking cooking pot. I guess my mother and father at this time were bending over backward to keep the family together in a better time-consuming way. We, as a team now, the eldest three, were once in a while getting into mischief around our hometown.

It was about two weeks before Halloween. The three of us, older kids, were walking about three or four blocks away from home, close to the local high school. We had started the daring game. Walking by a 6-plex building, where we knew some teachers lived. We dared each of us to enter the front door and push all the buttons that we could. We all dared each other. Off we walked and slowly approached the six-plex apartment building. We opened the door. Just inside the apartment, buttons were attached to a metal square. We all picked two buttons to push. Which we all did. We watched to see if anyone would come out of their apartment. Doors started to open, and almost everyone came out of their apartment. We laughed and dashed out of the door. We ran about a block, no body chased us. My older brother said, "Let's do it again."

The rest of us said, "No, you're kidding. No, it will be a double dare."

The oldest brother said, "Are you a chicken?"

We waited a while to let things settle. We then slowly walked by that same six-plex apartment building. The lights were still on. I said, "What if we were caught this time?"

My oldest brother said, "We won't get caught; we run too fast for them." So the plan was made, we slowly walked up to the apartment building.

Being very quiet, we opened the door and started to push the apartment buttons. Suddenly an apartment door opened very close to us, and a young man appeared. We ran quickly out the door, with this man chasing us. My older brother and sister sprang ahead of me; I couldn't keep up. That man was grabbing the back of my coat collar; he lifted me off the ground, my feet and legs were still running.

He walked me back to the apartment, where he said he was going to call the police. My whole body was shaking. Tears started to roll down my cheeks. Just the thought of my father coming down to the police station to pick me up. I was terrified. He started to ask me questions; I was so frozen in fright; I couldn't answer any questions. He asked me again, "How old are you?"

I didn't answer, but I just lowered my head in shame. Little did I know that this young man was a new teacher in the nearby high school. I suddenly spoke up, "We were on a double dare, and it was my older brother that was daring me to do this." Thank goodness this teacher knew a better solution. He took me with him; he knocked on every apartment door on the floor, where I apologized for what my brother and I had done. Thank goodness he let me go. Walking home, I met my brother and sister hiding behind a hedge, scared that the man would harm me.

I said, "See, what that double dare did to me? He was going to call the police and put me in jail." The three of us made a pact that we would never play that game again. But as the family grew, so did the idea of protecting each other and defending each other.

When the second boy was born, he seemed to be a brother who often ended up in trouble. I guess you could call him the black sheep of the family. He lived for excitement while the rest of us obeyed and conformed to proper behavior. This particular brother lived to unscramble and uproot the motto: "I will do what I want when I want to. I will do the double dare game as often as I want; they will never catch me running; I am the fastest runner in our street."

His most famous adventure really got him into turmoil. After playing tag in the school ground after school, the girl he was chasing ripped his good school shirt. She laughed at him; he ran after her so fast, she lost one of her shoes. This adventurist brother picked her shoe up and went around the neighborhood. He scooped up every pile of dog poop he could find and put it into her shoe. He then climbed up on an old backyard shed and placed her poop-filled shoe on the top of the roof.

Shortly after, us kids watched as we all hid behind a tree as the parents of the girl came into our neighborhood and canvassed the whole street looking for the house where my brother lived. First one house, then another. The parents were getting close. As kids, we peeked our heads around the corner to see them walk up our sidewalk to our front door. My father answered the door; he yelled for my brother, not once but three times. We pushed my brother away from behind the large tree. He had to face his dirty deed now. The parents and daughter, my father and brother went into the house. I wondered what was going to happen. We all started to wonder, will they put him in jail?

Soon our front door opened, and the parents and the daughter left. I wonder if he got the strap on his bum. This was a four-inch leather strap that hung inside the back of our cellar door. We later found out that an agreement had been made that the cost of the ripped shirt would equal the cost of a new pair of shoes. They were never to play with each other again.

Grade six for me was a real struggle. It was 1954; it was a different time. A time seniors can look back to their most eventful, unhappy, and sometimes happy times. This grade six experience was one of survival and a time that lifted my spirit to the highest point in the sky. In a small town, there is not much to get excited about. The week could consist of all the children going to school, the parents going to work, and the week would drag on, day after day. With the population of our town being 30,000 people, the pace of every day in our town seemed very slow.

And sometimes boring, for active children to be energetic children. Unfortunately, we had a grade six teacher with a very bad reputation. He was known to be uncaring and very mean-spirited. I was not happy to hear that I was to be placed in his grade six classroom. Having a teacher that did not like children like me always left a hurtful feeling in my heart. A feeling that I could not change. I had to withstand his eye glaring looks and mean actions that whole grade-six year. The fact that our new caring music teacher gave me a hopeful thought, that I had a chance to get away when it was time for our music lesson. It was a wonderful break when it came time for our music lesson. Our homeroom teacher had instilled disapproval or shame in every student that had to tolerate him.

Our music teacher radiated his love and care to every student he taught. For our grade six class, he was a ray of sunshine in our hearts. As music students, we hated the end of every music lesson. We wanted it to continue. But we were forced to return to a classroom with a teacher who would pick on us quite often. He showed no love and care for children; he should have never been a teacher; he will leave memories of hate for children to carry with them for years. I was one of those students who would quite often be picked by him to embarrass in front of the other students. Being from a large family that was poor and struggling in so many ways. My clothing was always a hand-me-down, with lots of wear and tear. I had a hole in one of my sweaters; my teacher said one day, "That sweater you're wearing; I think the hole should be in the back of your sweater."

Of course, my face turned beet red, every student around me looked at my sweater. This was a way to lower my self-esteem and make me feel ashamed and defeated in every way. This was a way to lash out at a child that he just didn't care about. He treated every student the same way. But I was his top pick to hurt on a daily basis. As a child, I felt helpless at times. But I knew this period of helplessness would soon disappear when I passed into grade seven.

I made a secret vow that this uncaring teacher would receive his hurtful treatment back to him. I later heard that this secret vow did come true for him. He had a severe stroke one day, which made him completely dependent on other people for his every need. His teaching career was over. Completely over. I hope he looks back on how his life now depended on people that I hope he treated with care or people that he daily put down and embarrassed. What comes around, goes around. Now, in my 75th year of age, this old saying does come true. I have personally seen it happen, time and time again. This unhappy, hurtful experience has stayed with me from the time I was 11 years old. Such a devastating memory must have been unforgettable to me as a child.

Sometimes unhappiness can soon turn into an unexpected joy in the life of a child. Our school received a very special music teacher, a teacher that loved and cared for children. He was a very enthusiastic teacher that could speak French and German and could sing opera. We thought that they had made a mistake by sending him here. He was just too good for our school. But we excitingly accepted him with open arms. He was a very easy-going and caring music teacher; he loved music and singing. He radiated his love of music to everyone he would meet. We didn't even have to sit at our desk for his lessons; we could sit on the floor, sit halfway on our desk, or just stand. He accepted everyone that tried out for our choir. It didn't matter if you were a boy or a girl; he accepted everyone that was willing to sing in his class. Because he showed his care and love for us, he soon became our special school idol.

We anxiously looked forward to having him for music. I think the school had made a mistake. This was exciting, just what all of us bored kids were looking for. He would play records and sing along with them; we would be sitting on our desks with our mouths open and our eyes admiring his melodious voice. Finally, you could hear happy music in our dull, bare school.

Finally, you could hear caring music coming from children that were happy with what they were doing in school. It didn't matter if you were a boy with a deep voice or a girl with an extra high-pitched voice; he encouraged and welcomed all voices for him to train. He encouraged music tunes and songs to come from your heart. It showed leadership and strength. He said all your voices matter. Even the male students took right to him. The boys learned to sing their hearts out. Tenor, soprano, or even alto. You were now a part of his group that he wanted to teach and instill the love of music to.

Mr. Blackman taught us two songs, one in French and the other in German. We were amazed that we could do that, and at home, we bragged that we were now learning French and German, whether our parents believed us, that was probably doubtful, but he was our new excitement, and as kids, we just loved him, because he cared about us.

Every year there was a contest for a school to win a large trophy for the best school choir. Our school had never won it, ever. In fact, they never even entered it, ever. We were the Protestant School—the Catholic Nun run school won it every year. And it was a well-known fact the catholic school kids would often brag that they were the best and would often throw rocks at us when we passed by their school; it was a constant battle between us.

Day after day, we practiced those two songs, sounds came out of those boys' mouths that I had never heard before. Mr. Blackman taught us to elevate our voices. The time came that Mr. Blackman told us he had entered us in the City School Choir Contest. We said we don't have a chance; we don't even have choir gowns, like the Catholic school choir. He said, "Never mind, you have the voices to win. And I will stand in front of you and direct you." He said we would sing our well-known French and German Songs. Well, we would have followed him to the moon, if he wanted us to. The day came when we hopped on the bus to go to the contest. Normally, all of us kids would have had a very doubtful feeling in the pit of our stomachs, but Mr. Blackman had given us a new adventure to look forward to. We were talking with each other, and it became quite loud on the bus.

Mr. Blackman said, "QUIET, PLEASE. I want all of you to visualize that you are there, and I am directing you; I want quiet now. I want you to save your voice for that very moment and then sing your heart out FOR ME." The whole bus was now quiet, and we arrived on time; we sat there and saw those Catholic School kids, all dressed in their fancy choir gowns, many I knew, and they were giggling and smirking at us. Especially at the boys in our choir. But we sat there quiet and very convinced that we were going to be teased by those Catholic School kids the following day.

It was time the Catholic School kids went first; boy they were good, but they never smiled; they were not happy at what they were singing. It was time for us to perform; we stood up and watched our teacher smile and laugh at us. We now felt at home. "Remember," he said, "sing your heart out, show how happy you are." Well, we did just that, first the song in French, then the song in German. You could see a white, pale look on the nun's face when we finished the last song.

You could hear a pin drop; it was so quiet. When Mr. Blackman stood in front of us and raised his arms. The sound that came out of our mouths that day, we will never forget. It blended together like one voice. Mr. Blackman was singing along with us.

Even though we sang in French and German, the sound was meaningful, both songs were Christmas Carols, and surely recognizable to everyone there. We all waited to hear that, of course, the Catholic School had won again. But it was just the opposite—the judges had picked us. WE WON! WE WON! The judges were so impressed with the two languages that we had sung in; they loved our singing. That trophy was ours now, for one whole year. We jumped back on that bus, and the excitement in us almost made that bus jump up and down. All the bus windows were opened, and we half hung out the windows, with loud cheering you could hear from where the bus left, to back to our school with our choir trophy sitting on Mr. Blackman's lap.

We had accomplished something that had never been done before. We won the City School Choir trophy because of that caring music teacher who gave us 'Love of Music' and that something extra.

When I think back on this memory, it was easy for me to remember. The sad memories I sometimes try to forget. But it is the happy memories that kept our family going. Our daily life continued, with the Protestant School kids now being able to brag and tease the Catholic School kids that we had won the school trophy. We continued throwing rocks at each other that was part of our battle that continued.

We received good and happy news for our family. Giving a helping hand to neighbors always pays off. A nickel or a penny is a reward that does not compare to the wonderful decision that our Salvation Army neighbor Captain made when he applied for my brothers and sisters to attend their summer camp for a week. His wife was the one that we always helped carry her groceries and parcels to her home and up the stairs.

Most of our neighbors knew it was becoming hard and expensive to have a family that continued to grow, and the needs kept on piling up. Or maybe they needed a break from all of us kids. Whatever the reason was, we as kids were jumping with joy. We had never ever been to camp or campfire. So it would be a week of extreme fun for all of us and a needed break for our parents. It would be another adventure I was sure we would never forget. We loved this couple for doing this for us. A week that our neighbors would miss our presence and sometimes mischief.

This Salvation Army couple was a very special part of our neighborhood. They were always helping people settle arguments and watching over the street in a caring and happy manner. He would be hiding behind his front door on Halloween to scare us. We were all ready to scare him. But he always had the ugliest mask and played the part to eventually scare us away until the next bunch of kids would approach his house.

After we would say, "You sure frightened us away." He would tell us he wasn't home that night. Who did you see at the house? It wasn't me. It was a couple that was loved and admired that lived on our street. Looking back in time, they sure were a kind memory that I haven't forgotten over all these years.

The day had come, and we were all ready and excited to go to the camp. The bus ride took us away from a family situation that was taking us into a stressful and uncaring world. A world that we as children just couldn't change but wanted to from the depths of our hearts. We wanted our past family situation to return when we used to laugh and have fun with each other.

The bus ride was a long one, but each child was full of excitement, knowing they were on their way to a week where they could be themselves and share each day with others, knowing all they had to do was have fun and more fun. We sang songs, talked and cheered when we saw cows and horses in the countryside, especially if we hadn't seen them before. We had the bus window open; the smell of the real country side filled our nostrils. Cool, fresh air was a sign that the camp was near. The adults on the bus joined in on our fun. I will never forget arriving at the camp. The bus driver honked and joined in on the fun; he honked his horn to let everyone at the camp know that we were here.

Departing the bus with our attached name tags and numbers, we all headed for the swings. The camp counselors rounded us up. The young counselors showed us around, we laughed, and they showed us their love and care for us. Camp counselors showed us the wooden clad cabins with bunk beds. Right then and there, we started to pick which bunk we wanted, the high one or the lower one. You could tell the young counselors were feeling the excitement we were showing, and they showed their love in return. We all laughed together, and as a group of deserving children, we felt at that time we had become one.

The time I spent at the camp is a time that will always stay with me. A memory that took me away from a situation that was daily becoming very stressful. I'm sure all the children on that bus were well-deserving in some way. They were just so happy to be away from their own family problems. We were all one now, there to have fun and share our togetherness in a childlike way. Of course, there were rules, but each child was glad to pitch in and make sure our time together resulted in a closeness. That coming from a family with multiple children, I never hardly experienced a time to make close friends that were not my brother or sister. A time to reflect on what a child was, running games, sharing a cabin with new friends, swinging on the swings, swimming, singing songs at a nighttime campfire, all cuddled close and feeling you never wanted this experience to end.

Now, as an adult, when I pass by a red kettle to collect money at Xmas time from the Salvation Army, I remember the one week of fun that they gave me that summer, and whatever I have on me that day, I make sure I put it in the kettle.

After arriving home from the Summer Camp, we again had to settle into a family situation, that at times, was very hurtful in the ears and heart of our very soul. After experiencing welcoming, fun, and happy times at the camp, it was a real letdown. It was still summer, and we as children still had the freedom of going outside, and getting away from household family fights.

When nobody expected it, the weather surprised everyone turning its power into Hurricane Hazel. Where we lived, in a two-story stucco home, a very large tree had been planted probably 70 to 80 years ago. A tree as a child, I could not put both arms around and touch the end of its circumference. A tree that stood strong and mighty from the time I was born. It was always there for me as a child to hug, crawl into its above-ground roots, arising from the ground, carving my initials into its bark. We have always shared our presence with this wonderful tree of life.

In fact, this very tree saved our home and saved our lives from the force of Hurricane Hazel. I will never forget the day Hurricane Hazel came roaring through our guarded hometown. Back in those days, there was no warning that they had to inform the community. It was up to you to watch the weather conditions if they were unusual like, very strong winds, a sudden temperature drop, and an abnormal dark sky. Common sense should have told you to get into a safe shelter. But there were none of these conditions when my brothers and sisters and I decided to take a trip to the public swimming pool that would have shown us what was heading our way.

We had left our home and had traveled up the street, where the Catholic School ground was situated. We had walked about halfway across the playground when we heard our mother call for us to come home. Her calling us was unusual because we already told her where we were going. But just the tone of her call was far more serious. I wanted to continue, but my sister said, "No! Let's go back." The wind had increased to the point that it was picking up the top layer of the ground dirt. After arriving home, our mother told us there was going to be a bad storm ahead. She didn't tell us how she knew. When I think back to this time, I knew she had a mother's intuition that something bad was about to happen.

We all huddled together into a tiny closet in my parents' bedroom. My father was not home. He was working in the United States at that time. At these times, we looked for him to have complete safety. The wind suddenly became very strong. We could hear our very large and old maple tree in our front lawn being hit by the strength of the wind. The base six to nine ft. in circumstance our maple tree that stood strong and high on our front lawn, you could hear the swaying of the large branches. We could hear some of its branches cracking and hitting the side of our house. This maple tree already hovering over the street lights and taking over half of our front lawn, I'm sure, was taking a beating. It was a majestic, hardy tree that had earned its place on our street to stand mighty; hearing the roar of a speeding freight train made our family cuddle even closer.

We were still huddled together in a closet. We could hear blow-away objects hitting our house. Our neighborhood contained homes that were fairly close together with just a walkway on both sides. Our backyards were the same size, down the block, about 125 ft. long. A backyard size that is unheard of in today's world. The roaring fast, freight train sound continued, it was so loud, it was almost deafening. For us cuddled in the closet, it seemed it would never stop. But then the rain came down in torrents.

And then it was quiet. The most peaceful quiet I can remember. We stayed huddled in the closet while my mother ventured out to look out of the bedroom window. All we heard her say was, Oh my God! over and over again.

Her hands went to her mouth, covering it, but still uttering 'Oh My God!' She told us to stay where we were until she would call us. She left the bedroom, for some strange reason our bedroom window had not blown out or shattered. She was gone quite a while, investigating the damage that this storm had caused. She called us to come out, and we could only look out the windows.

Our home had not been touched. Although, we had heard many objects being thrown up against it. There were tree branches and debris everywhere on our street. Cars had been pushed over, flattened, and some had been completely turned on their side. We were not to leave the house until our father had returned from the United States. Concrete steps had been pulled away from the homes they stood in front of. Aside from our hometown, I could only imagine the destruction this Hurricane could cause in our neighborhood, fruit-producing open land.

Well, like many times over and over again, in our hometown, we all came together to help each other in any way that we could. Our strength and united care as a community that often faced these life-changing obsoletes, almost sometimes too much to bear, would stand united. Which we did, and within a year, you would have never known, this hurricane and swept through our community.

Soon I found myself in junior high school grades seven and eight. A time in a young person's life when you open up to who you are. A time when how your appearance has changed from a clumsy, carefree girl to now a young woman. At times we had to put on a front for the rest of the world. Our family was struggling in so many ways. My father rarely worked, was home often, and started to drink. His fatherly happiness had turned to hatred. He found himself unemployed, having mental problems, useless, and unhappy that he now had so many people depending on him to keep things running.

I will never forget the day I was in my grade eight class schoolroom. When a call came over the phone for me to go to the principal's office. My father was sitting in the chair, along with the principal across from him. My father was complaining that I and my sister were given too much homework from school, and as children, we didn't have enough time to saw wood in the basement for the large, old wood furnace that we had to heat our home. I could hardly believe he would do such a thing. His mental state had changed dramatically. How embarrassed I was. In fact, it left me stunned and speechless. I guess he was jealous of us enjoying junior high school. He was definitely there to hurt our feelings and embarrass us in so many ways. The funny part was the principal agreed with my father. My face turned beet red, and tears came down my face.

The teenage happiness that I was proudly enjoying and displaying had fallen to the floor with a hurtful crash. My father had warned that if this continued, he would take us out of the school to now complete household duties. I looked at my father's face; I could see this wasn't my real father inside this person I once called Daddy.

Three weeks later, he told me and my sister that we were needed at home to look after household duties. That was a time I felt like I was in prison camp. He had the two of us scrub floors, cook, do laundry, etc. My mother was home but by now had become scared to speak up against him.

My mother's self-esteem had worn down to almost nothing. Within a week, the Children's Aid Society stepped in. A young woman approached my sister and me and asked us very meaningful and helpful questions. Did we miss school? Were we happy? Thank goodness for her stepping in. Within a week, my sister and I were back at school. I think the teachers at that school realized we were having a bad environment to contend with.

We were in home studies class, each class had to make a potholder, an apron, and a skirt to finish and pass this class. Not being able to buy material for any of these items to make made us stand out from the other kids. My sister, Cheryl, and I had to find some way to get material. We took apart an old table cloth to make our potholder and apron. To this day, I love the care that my home studies class teacher gave us. She took off her own time and bought material for Cheryl and me to make a skirt. She personally took the time to give us instructions on how to make a skirt. I will always remember her kindness.

We had reached the end of the year for our junior high school. The prom was fast approaching. My sister, Cheryl, and I knew there was no way we could have attended. We needed to have a new dress and a new pair of shoes. We pulled each other aside at school one day. We made a vow that when we were adults, we would have our own prom to attend. This made the time approaching the prom not hurt so much when everyone else was talking about going. There was a girl about five houses away from us. I'm sure she didn't realize the hurt that we were feeling inside when she would approach us and show us her new dress and pair of shoes. We had to make an excuse, so we used my father's hurtful behavior, telling everyone we weren't allowed to go. That for sure is a memory that I wish I could have changed from heartbreaking to looking forward to having and enjoying a wonderful grade eight graduation prom. Life brings disappointments and hurt, but you lift your head high, and continue on, knowing that you always have the love of your brothers and sisters to lean on.

Passing into grade nine was a real acknowledgment form e. My junior high school was stressful, but it was all now behind me. Now I had high school to try and conquer. This school building stood mighty and tall; three-stories tall, massive to look at. Back in those days, we only had one high school, so all those children from families, usually large families, had now to fit into one school. It was an old building, with gyms. And training facilities and even a stage for high school assemblies and plays. By now, my oldest brother Carl had reached Grade 11 and Grade 12 in high school.

The situation had not changed at all at home. In fact, it had become worse. We all walked on broken eggshells at home. A horrible environment to live in. With our family slowly breaking apart. We, as children, clung to times that we shared our love and caring for each other. Our neighbors, of course, did everything they could to help. One neighbor that was elderly knew my oldest brother Carl was taking car mechanics in high school. He didn't drive anymore. He offered his car to the high school for free for the students to work on. The stipulation was if they got it running, it would be given to my brother, Carl, free of charge.

Having the same neighbors, year after year, they have watched us growing up from birth. Time passes, and life goes on, and you have to deal with what life provides for you. This neighbor knew and realized that our family was struggling in many ways. This was his kindness that gave all of us as children a reason to believe that there is care in the heart of some people, and the fact that he was willing to do this, I'm sure he thought it would help the whole family in some way.

Months later, I will never forget my brother, Carl, came driving down our home town street, where we lived; he was honking the horn driving the neighbor's car with the Mechanic school teacher and three other boys in the back of our neighbor's old car that he had given to the high school. That wonderful, giving neighbor across the street from us ran to the car, clapping. He was overjoyed and surprised that the school had good use of it and got it running. It was now my brother's car, free of charge. A gift that my brother will never forget.

Now my brother had something special that many rich kids didn't have. He had his own car that he and his classmates had worked on just for him. It was, I'm sure, the biggest morale boaster that he had ever well earned. That same car became a safe haven for him. Soon after, my father and oldest brother Carl were fighting verbally, which later erupted into a physical fight.

Our family all knew that my brother, Carl, and my father were not speaking or connecting paths. My brother, Carl, disappeared in that special old car one day with another runaway friend. I guess they both had decided that they just had to get away from their unhappy homes. They traveled north in tobacco country, and both of them worked on farms for money and a place to stay. My father, in his altered state, never wanted to report them missing, but my mother went directly to the police and reported them missing.

During this time, the last baby was born now and turned three years old. So now we are a family of eight children. Four boys and four girls. I often admired families with just one child or two. Those families were happy and thriving. I guess I was jealous and wanted to be in their family environment. I think if our family situation was different and our environment wouldn't have fallen apart, I would not feel this way. But I should be thankful for what I have, the love and care of my brothers and sisters, and all the happy, memorable times that we shared together.

With me and my sister, Cheryl, now in grade nine, and my brother, Carl, nearing his grade 12 graduation, our home situation had not changed, in fact, it was far worse. Knowing you have to attend high school with old hand-me-down clothes that now had become old-fashioned always left me with low self-esteem. I just didn't have the family happiness in my heart anymore. Life was such a struggle for all of us. But it was my oldest brother Carl that tried to step up and be the head of the household. With my father interfering in every way he could. My uncle and aunt would send us money every once in a while. This would be without my father knowing. My brother would constantly tell me to stay in school but not having appropriate clothing and cost of books. Back in those days, you had to pay for your high school books. But knowing past high school students, I was able to pick up their used books for just my babysitting money.

Everyone seemed to gather high school friends. But I must have shown my struggle and unhappiness on my face; I guess no one wanted to become friends with a teenager that really didn't show an outward sign of success. I couldn't really bring any friends home; my father would greet them with an unwelcome greeting for sure, usually a drunken one. Any extra time I had, I had to look after my own brothers and sisters. Or I would be out babysitting other children to earn money for the household. The teenage happiness that everyone else had, I just didn't have it. I felt my teenage years were full of worries.

My brother, Carl, now had a chance to apply to a car manufacturing plant to start his journey as a money-making person in our family. My sister, Betty, two years older than me, soon joined him at the same plant, also working on the kid line. This opportunity made a real difference in our financial needs as a family. The third and fourth oldest children really didn't have a chance of having a real teenage experience. Often, we were invited to homes of other friends. But we never had the chance of having friends over because of my father's mean, uncaring behavior, who would yell at them.

We were all growing up, the youngest three years old. With the third and fourth oldest, babysitting, fruit picking, anything we could do to bring money into the home. My father's mother had a large section of land that often helped us out. She grew vegetables, fruit, and other items.

I was now hoping that I could hang in there and try and finish high school, but having to wear hand-me-down clothes that were old-fashioned, dampened my enthusiasm and put me into a class of students they called the poor students or the nerds. Babysitting gave me a chance to visit other homes that I often wished I'd lived in. These homes had plenty of food to eat, nice clothes, and a happy atmosphere. My oldest brother Carl often insisted that I stay in school. But it was such a struggle for me.

I made it to finish grade 11 and then got a job as a waitress and short-order cook in a small coffee shop. I saved my money for two years and went to Business College. I then got a part-time job working as a receptionist for a chiropractor. Striving to get ahead, I then got a full-time job as a secretary in a real estate office. Working hard to get ahead, I then passed my real estate license with a score of 86. Well, then I really needed a car. I had no money for a car, so I borrowed $900.00 from the bank to buy a 1966 white rambler. I was shaking in my boots. I now owed the bank $900.00. To me, that was so much money, how could I ever pay it back? It for sure kept me up a few nights. That was such a huge amount of money. But I did pay it back. Off I would drive to make more money, to someday buy a new car. This time I didn't have to borrow any money from the bank.

My father realized that his own children were now taking over the importance of his job as a money-making father, SO HE LEFT US, YES, ALL EIGHT OF US AND MY MOTHER. But, by now, my brother, Carl, and sister, Cheryl, were working in the car manufacturing plant, and me, now working in real estate, we pooled our money and set up our own family where we could now look after ourselves and our financial needs. We finally were able to live like other families. There was now happiness in our home. Our need to get ahead was still the top priority in our family. Our most common saying was "Strong together, we can be," "New ways for us to smile together as one."

Our mother slowly regained her lost self-esteem and happily remarried a wonderful man that now accepted all of us as his new family. The three oldest children are now on their own. With five children, my mother and new stepfather, creating a family that is still very close and living a life that they always deserved.

For some, a hometown is just a place. But for many, it is part of what they were and what they have become. It was their birthplace, how they grew up as a child, how their environment shaped their thinking and decision-making. A house is a house, but for many, that just means a place that you live in. When you say, I sure miss home, that means your comfort place, our safe place, a place that just makes you feel wanted and loved. There's no other place in this world that you can say I sure miss my hometown. It's where your friends are that you grew up with and went to school with. It's a place that you want to return to when you are unsure of yourself and want that inner strength that you always knew you had in your hometown.

When I think back on my life, I often wonder how I turned all that hate and self-esteem-draining family brokenness into a person. A person that fought back in every way to be accepted, loved, and admired. Always striving to fight my way to the top, to be who I was, to be the person I deserved to be. The fact that I came from a family that was poor, I had to push that aside.

I think it taught me that I had to have a fighting will and spirit to show everyone that I was just as important and smart as they were. Strong together, we can be. May my memories live on in the heart of the family I leave behind. Am I thankful for the life that I had? YOU BET I AM! What can be more important than life? My family was not the best, but what we shared together cannot compare with the love and experiences we lived as one. Brothers and sisters, always sharing our life together. Revisiting the most memorable recalls of our past memory, let them always warm my heart. Let the sun shine down on my hometown, and warm the hearts of everyone there.

Life doesn't always begin and end with happily ever after. That might be true for very few families in today's world. Embracing and knowing love and happiness in a family. Then feeling and watching this happiness slowly disappear leaves a deep hurtful feeling in any child's heart. The safety that a child has when they know their family is happy can then turn to sadness, fear, and mistrust and can eventually have a child stand back, and slowly lose their openness to the world. They slowly start to lose their stand-alone self-esteem.

Now many of us are in our seventies and under. But it was me, Abbey, the third oldest in the family that was willing to tell the story of my family's journey. Our spirit and will to survive and stand together became our main goal after our father left us all. Yes, he left all of his eight children and his wife to now survive on their own. To tell you it was devastating and unbelievable is an understatement. His love of liquor and his unwillingness to get help for his mental problems had reached such an extent that it seemed beyond his control. It was now time that it gave us children and mother a chance to show the world that we could survive. He was dragging our family into a world of fear and unhappiness that we never knew.

With the help of some old neighbors and our willing spirit, we now had every day that was free from his new harmful drunken journey. Our love and closeness that we shared would make our attempt to free ourselves of his constant hurt and interference. 'We are strong, we are mighty,' was our slogan to push ahead and have a caring future ahead of us.

Life does not let you know what your journey will be. Accept each day, and honor its beginning and end. Know that there could be happiness and sadness in each emotional hill that you have to climb. Your new day will be a day that you look back on in your memory. Memories are all that we have left; when we make that last journey home, to our beloved 'Hometown.'

A story has to have an end. But my story will never end. Life is a continual gift that is treasured. Whatever you face in life is never promised or just given. A wonderful beginning, and for our family, it will never end, I hope. Our children and grandchildren will live on to tell the meaningful story of their hometown.

Was my time on this earth valuable to me? Was it a time that I could smile, was it a time that I could cry? Was it a time that I could be thankful that I was here to live it? YOU BET IT WAS!

My family has all grown up now; we are all still close. Very involved in our community. Still watch over our hometown, and look forward to passing on our story to our children and grandchildren. All different in their own way. Sharing their talents and personalities within our hometown.

I may not have mentioned my brothers and sisters by name too much in this story, but they are what this story is all about. I wanted you to know how they turned their lives into being caring and involved citizens in our hometown. Proud is not a strong enough word to express how I am overjoyed at how they became a pillar of our community and now have a family themselves to continue their story.

From the youngest to the oldest

Robbie – Male – He had three sons – Policeman – Security

Missy – Female – She had two children – R N. Nurse for years – recently retired

Gary – Male – He had two children – Welder – Passed away at age 56

Jed – Male – He had six children – Handyman

Cheryl – Female – She had four children – head of Laundry – Old age home

Abbey – Female – had one child – short-order cook, Lab tech, Data Entry, secretary, writer

Betty – Female – She had two children – Car plant worker

Carl – Male – He had one child, car plant worker

Our 21 grandchildren will be thrilled to pass on their stories to honor the hometown they shared with the world.

But time goes on, and my special hometown has grown up, and I have grown up too, now I am old and cherish my thoughts of what my hometown meant to me. My memory sometimes fades, so it was very important to write this story, so I would always be able to have someone read it to me when my memory becomes diminished. The dream of our hometown has no limits. Let the glow of that memory forever stay with me. I am privileged to share this memory with you because, for some, this could have been your hometown too.